For:

D1005677

You're My Friend Be Claus

By Susie Schick-Pierce
and Jean Schick-Jacobowitz

Illustrated by Wendy Wallin Malinow

PETER PAUPER PRESS, INC.
WHITE PLAINS, NEW YORK

*For Garrett and Phil, and our
special families and friends*

Copyright © 1996
Susie Schick-Pierce, Jean
Schick-Jacobowitz, and
Wendy Wallin Malinow
Published by
Peter Pauper Press, Inc.
202 Mamaroneck Avenue
White Plains, NY 10601
All rights reserved
ISBN 0-88088-803-2
Printed in China
7 6 5 4 3 2 1

The best present you can receive is true friendship. Friendship is magical, joyous, uncritical, and loving. And if you've been a good friend all year, Santa will surely bring you friendship in return.

You're My Friend

BeClaus

Being Friends with You Makes it easy to believe in Christmas

You're My Friend

BeClaus

By loving the
ORDINARY
you make it

EXTRAORDINARY

You're My Friend

Be Claus

You have given
in ways only
the heart
can see

You're My Friend

BeClaus

You give with
your whole
unprotected
heart

You're My Friend
Be Claus

Each holiday season
your FRIENDSHIP
grows more precious
and valuable

You're My Friend

BeClaus

You know Love
lives on beyond
the holidays

You're My Friend

Be Claus

FEELINGS bring us
together...
though we may be
miles apart

You're My Friend
BeClaus

You know; what we get
FROM Christmas is
much more valuable
Than what we get
FOR Christmas

You're My Friend

BeClaus

You show me by
giving from your HEAR
- you really understand
Christmas

You're My Friend

BeClaus

You know—
FRIENDSHIP keeps no
record of rights
and wrongs

ughty · nice · naughty · nice ·
naughty · nice · naughty · nice
aughty · nice · naughty · nice ·

You're My Friend

Be Claus

You know how to
live life
Without growing old

You're My Friend
Be Claus

You give of yourself
not just to family
and friends
but to everyone

You're My Friend

Be Claus

You're always
there
to lean on

You're My Friend

Be Claus

Your
SMILE
warms my
world

BeClaus

You always tell me I
look wonderful
(in spite of all my
nooks and crannies)

You're My Friend

BeClaus

You accept the
world as it is
Weeds and all

You turn burdens
into adventures

You're My Friend

Be Claus

You're full of
ENERGY
a loving energy

You're My Friend
Be Claus

You know, the most
significant gifts
can't be put under a tree
or wrapped up in a box

You're My Friend

BeClaus

Deeds of CARING
Become more
precious over
time

You're My Friend

BeClaus

You turn my
FAILURES
into SUCCESSES

You're My Friend
Be Claus

You touch my
heart
without knowing it

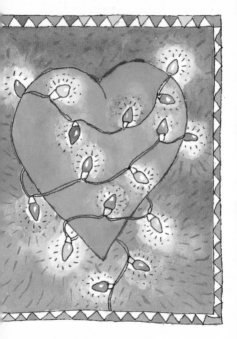

You're My Friend

Be Claus

You know: You've
got to do some
heart and soul giving
To really understand
Christmas

You're My Friend

BeClaus

You encourage me
to do things
that seem
impossible

You're My Friend

BeClaus

You give me a
FRIENDSHIP
that is magical

You're My Friend

Be Claus

You Jingle
my spirit
when I am
down and out

You're My Friend

BeClaus

You love
the
un-loveable

You're My Friend

BeClaus

Those who have real
Christmas feelings
Those who get most from
it one day a year
Are those who give the
most to everyone
throughout the year

JANUARY ☆ FEBRUARY ☆ MARCH
APRIL ☆ MAY ☆ JUNE ☆ JULY ☆
AUGUST ☆ SEPTEMBER ☆ OCTOBER
GO TO THE SHELTER
4
5 FIND DOG'S OWNER
6
7
9 TAKE FOOD TO SHELTER
10
11 HELP JANE'S MOM
12
SEE JOHN
14
15
16
17
19
20 FUNDRAISER 8:00
21 PACK UP OLD CLOTHES.
22
24
25
26
27

You're My Friend

BeClaus

My most
precious gift
from you
is you

You're My Friend

BeClaus

JuST
BeClaus
You're
You!

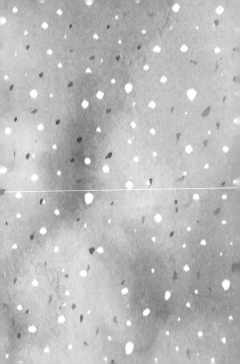